Pains

Tears and Shadows

- Victims of War Tell Their Stories -

By

Felix N Odiogor-Odoh

DEDICATION

Dedicated to: My wife, Olukemi.

My children, Faith, Favour, Felicity and Joy.

My mother Lucy, and to all who suffered

as war victims all over the world.

Disclaimer and Publication Notice

While all attempts have been made to verify information provided in this publication, the author assumes no responsibility to errors, omissions, or contrary interpretation of the subject matter therein. The author disclaims any warranties (expressed or implied), merchantability or fitness for any purpose.

This publication is not intended for use as a source of legal or accounting advice. The author wants to stress that the information contained herein may be subject to varying state and/or local laws or regulations. All users are advised to retain competent counsel to determine what state or local laws or regulation may apply to the user's particular business.
The purchaser or reader of this publication assumes responsibility for the use of the materials and information.

The author and publisher do not warrant the performance of effectiveness of any sites stated in this book. All links are for information and educational purposes only and are not warranted for content, accuracy or any other implied or explicit purpose. Adherence to all applicable laws and regulations, federal or state, and local governing professional licensing, business practices, advertising and all other aspects of doing business in any jurisdiction is the sole responsibility of the purchaser or reader. The author assumes no responsibility or liability whatsoever on behalf of any purchaser or reader of this material.

ACKNOWLEDGMENTS

I wish to acknowledge the help and support of all who contributed to make this book and its publication possible. I thank God for the inspiration.

Introduction

This is more than an ordinary story book, it is real life experiences of actual human beings and it is intended to educate, inform and help everyone who reads it . I perceive that it might help many war victims unburden lifelong pain that had trailed them all through life.

There are many costs and effects of war that are never calculated or realized; there are many sides of armed conflicts that are never revealed when people go to war. The costs of war to any people are enormous and many of them go unnoticed, unaddressed and usually lingers throughout a life time without the sufferers sometimes being aware of what is happening to them. It is not that people want it that way or that they are unforgiving, but the fact is that most times, scares don't go away.

I have heard people yearning for a war, one case in mind was before the Libyan civil war when some of the major actors were boasting on national television about war, and I felt sorry for them. I am sure they know better now. It was the same in Iraq in 1990 and in Ivory Coast, Kenya and many other places. War destroys, robs people of loved ones, and creates enmity, humiliation, anger and frustration in people. The society is usually at the receiving end of all these bad effects of war.

Chapter One

War and its effects

United Nation Declaration on Human Right

States:

Article 1. All human beings are born free and equal in dignity and rights. They are endowed with reason and conscience and should act towards one another in a spirit of brotherhood.

Article 2. Everyone is entitled to all the rights and freedom set forth in this Declaration, without distinction of any kind, such as race, colour, sex, language, religion, political or other opinion, national or social origin, property, birth or other status. Furthermore, no distinction shall be made on the basis of the political, jurisdictional or international status of the country or territory to which a person belongs, whether it be independent, trust, non-self-government or under any other limitation of sovereignty.

Article 3. Everyone has a right to life, liberty and security of person

Article 4. No one shall be held in slavery or servitude; slavery and slave trade shall be prohibited in all their forms.

Article 5. No one shall be subject to torture or to cruel, inhuman or degrading treatment or punishment.

Article 6. Everyone has the right to recognition everywhere as a person before the law.

Article 7. All are equal before the law and are entitled without any discrimination to equal protection of the law. All are entitled to equal protection against any discrimination in violation of this Declaration and against any incitement to such discrimination."

(http://www.un.org/en/documents/udhr/)

The above United Nation Human Right Declaration is intended to help people live and pursue their endeavour wherever they choose to live. However, it is openly violated and the result of such actions are the burdens we see in the testimonies of people who testified of their experiences in this book.

Why people go to war

There are many reasons on why people go to war. War certainly means different things to different people. The act of aggression is very difficult to explain and the only people who can explain it are the principal actors in any particular situation but unfortunately, many of them never come true with their real motives for going to war because it might not be reasonable enough. In the bid to mobilize people for war, many substances and the original causes of the conflict are left out and secondary reasons set in. However, there are obvious reasons why a war might have happened; these include:

Wars are caused by things such as border disagreement, fighting for resources, and territorial invasion by other countries. War is also caused by differences in policies and also provocative acts such as terrorism and arrests of other nationals." (http://uk.ask.com)

Religion has been a major cause of conflict in the world both in the past and at present. Religious intolerance leads to bloodletting and war.

Political intolerance can lead to conflicts and destruction of lives and properties, such conflicts occur when people fail to agree on the result of elections and make demands which the other people concerned will never concede.

Anger starts war. Generally, war is a result of a national entity wishing to improve the standard of living for its people" (http://wiki.answers.com)

Wars happen when the parties involved in a conflict fail to reach agreement, abide by or enforce an agreement over a difference. This happens if efforts have been made to resolve lingering demands causing a conflict situation, like it happened in Falkland Islands, Kuwait and Nigeria.

A nation can go to war to protect its people and its sovereignty, if it feels threatened by others who want to invade these exclusive rights that it has among nations.

Wars happen when people feel that the gains from such conflict will be greater than the sacrifice they will make, be it material or human lives.

There are many other reasons that can be proffered for conflicts leading to war. We are majorly concerned with the effects of war on people during and long after the war is over.

Psychological effects of war

A lot of people suffer psychological effects long after a war is over; these include soldiers, both serving and retired; civilians, young and old. It is unfortunate that in many cases little or no effort is made to address these problems, and this leads to sad consequences.

According to William Little "More Falklands veterans have committed suicide than were killed during the conflict. More than five times the number of British troops killed in the last Gulf war have also committed suicide. Research by Shelter reveals that one in four homeless people are ex armed services personnel. Thousands live rough or in sheltered accommodation. Many also suffer from drug and alcohol abuse. Returning armed services personnel often end up in rehab, on the streets or with severe mental health problems. Nearly 5,000 ex-servicemen are in prison, often as a result of the trauma suffered in war." (PeaceMatters: www.ppu.org.uk)

Effects of War on Children

According to UNICEF, "In times of conflict, children are always the most vulnerable. Right now, millions of children around the world are caught up in conflicts where they are not just bystanders, but targets. In South Sudan, Sudan, and Central African Republic, thousands of young people are being recruited and exploited as child soldiers. Elsewhere, children suffer from the extreme effects of armed conflicts, exposing them to hunger, disease, injury, psychological trauma and sexual exploitation" (UNICEF: Children in conflict, Nov. 2012)

Effects of war on women

Women suffer untold hardship and humiliation during and after war, no matter how small. Apart from the fact that members of her family might be involved in the battle; a woman is very vulnerable when war takes place. Women had been targets for sexual abuse; many women were usually violently raped and maltreated by soldiers and civilians. Women, who in many cases were unarmed, could be captured, tortured and led away captive. In many war situations, soldiers burn down buildings and leave women and children exposed to bad weather conditions with no food or water.

According to Lucinda March, "Women and children account for almost 80% of the casualties of conflict and war as well as 80% of the 40 million people in world who are now refugees from their homes. It is one of the unspoken facts of militarism that women often become the spoils of war, their deaths are considered collateral damage and their bodies are frequently used as battlegrounds and as commodities that can be traded." "Sexual violence as a tool of war has left hundreds of thousands of women raped, brutalized, impregnated and infected with HIV/AIDS. And hundreds of thousands of women are trafficked annually for forced labor and sexual slavery. Much of this trafficking is to service western troops in brothels near military bases. Even women serving in the military are subjected to sexual violence." (Unacceptable: The Impact of War on Women and Children, CommonDreams.org 2004)

Writing on "civilians in war zones, Women and children worst," Much Butchery said, "In Bosnia, tens of thousands of women were raped; in eastern Congo in recent years some 80% of fistula cases reported in women are thought to be the result of such crimes. High numbers of similar cases were reported from Burundi, Chad, Congo, Sierra Leone and Liberia, according to the Geneva-based Centre for the Democratic Control of Armed Forces. An estimated 70% of

Rwanda's rape survivors were infected with HIV." (The Economist Newspaper 2014)

Chapter Two

The Wind of War

This book contains real live stories of people who had various experiences of war from different parts of the world. The stories are from people of different age, social leaning and academic backgrounds. These stories tell what happens when the shellings are on and when they are over. They are stories of what happens to people when the soldiers are there and when they are gone.

While people die and suffer as a result of war, many of those who started it, according to some stories I read, send their families overseas, far from any heat of trouble. They mobilise other people for war while playing safe with their own families. Many of the rulers and their aides dine and wine while the "patriots" are hurting and dying. They are quite glad to hire tugs and miscreants to promote war; their paid staff and beneficiaries are always busy manipulating and mounting propaganda to promote their course. For example, BBC News, Friday May 9, 2014, stated the cause of war in South Sudan as "The violence began when President Kilr accused his sacked deputy Mr Machar, of plotting a coup. Mr Machar denied the allegation but marshalled a rebel army to fight the government" (BBC News, World, May 2014). The BBC News quoted a UN report as saying "'Widespread and systematic' atrocities had been carried out by both side in homes, hospitals, mosques, churches and UN compounds"

According to Anirudh et al, "The impact of war-related stressors may occur as the direct result of physical and visual impact, media exposure, or through the various forms of interpersonal experience – the wounding and killing of loved ones, disease and emotional contagion, and social disruption and loss of peer related experience, routinized family, school and community life. In some instances, children may be kidnapped and forced to participate as child warriors in violent acts under the threat of losing their lives" (Anirudh Purwar, Arnab Dhabal and Diptarka Chakravarty: Psychological effects of War and Terrorism on children)

Many people in Europe, Asia, Africa or America, who long for political power want to get it by all means including dragging their nations to armed conflicts and bloodletting but one thing everyone must know is that many of them are never direct victims of war.

People suffer long after the battles are over and usually they are left on their own to bear the brunt. They are never given adequate support to get over the horror brought on them by those they trusted to provide security for them. People get agitated, angry, frustrated and wrecked. Hopelessness and insecurity are consequences of war. Warmongers usually get away with their atrocities, encouraging others to perpetrate the same in future. There are always many of causalities that are unaccounted for after the war.

Many of these stories in this book may affect you in several ways; they can influence, inform and help impact your decisions when war situations seems likely. They can placate your "injured existence" and make you resolve to give life a second chance, to succeed. They can help you not to succumb to the wimps and caprices of warmongers. Knowing that there are people who are like you all over the world, who made it after surviving the war can motivate you to help others who are passing through "after war traumas", survive their fears and pains no matter how long they have borne the burden. There are many who I wished contributed their experience to this book, but they didn't, they couldn't bear reliving their experiences. I salute the courage of those who contributed to this work. Only little editing was done on the stories so that their originality is maintained, and the names remains anonymous for various reasons.

Chapter Three

Testimony one

I call it 'The ill-fated year', It was the year 1971, 'This tragic year marks the breakup of my beloved country Pakistan into two separate parts. Till my last breath I will not be able to forget this most unfortunate chapter of my life. I was a happily married woman living in the beautiful city of Lahore. My younger brother's wedding was to take place in a few months so I was preparing to leave for Rawalpindi (another city) where my parents resided. Eager, excited and completely unaware of the worst to come.

At this time there was already a great deal of political unrest going on between East and West Pakistani for several months. The candidate in East Pakistan had won the election with vast majority. However; the strongest candidate in West

Pakistan along with military high officials continued to keep the winning candidate deprived off his rightful opportunity of becoming the Prime minister of the state. This injustice along with foreign propaganda lead to the vilest disobedience movement.

As the movement became stronger; things started getting worse. The enemy neighboring country 'India' got its opportunity of centuries, when it saw this civil war, of destabilizing our country. It was the best time for them to attack Pakistan. The government ordered to evacuate the city of Lahore since it was severely under the threat of being attacked.

We have to leave Lahore,' my husband told me. It was totally unexpected.

Where and why,' I asked in disbelief, with my eyes wide open.

We will have to migrate to Rawalpindi in a day or two, leaving everything behind, Lahore is under a threat of being attacked,' he told me.

Left with no other choice, I left the house of my dreams along with my husband. Since a lot of families were moving from the city it was quite hard to find a suitable means of transport.

After a tiresome wait my husband made arrangements for us to travel to Rawalpindi by road in a bus.

The tortuous and tiresome journey began but the worst was yet to come. The thought of leaving my house and city was nerve wracking, so I tried thinking about my parents and siblings in Rawalpindi to comfort myself. While I was lost, deeply in my thoughts; our bus was crossing the bridge of River Ravi (The Bridge that separates the city of Lahore from rest of the country) when the horrific bombarding began. There was chaos in the bus. No one knew what happened. The traffic stopped on the bridge and I could see fighter planes trying to destroy the bridge by bombarding it.

What's going on?' 'What's going on?' I shouted.

Heads down! 'Kneel down everybody!' the driver shouted.

India has attacked Lahore,' 'they will destroy us,' 'Help us O Lord,' I could hear several voices at a time.

I started reciting my final prayers along with other passengers on the bus since any strike could take our life. Those were the most intense moments of my entire life. Death stood just a step away. My husband and I held hands forcefully ensuring that we die together.

O Lord! Please save us and forgive us and protect our country from enemies,'

The shelling continued but every time the fighter missed its target, 'The Bridge'

It was the Indian army trying to sweep away the bridge since it was the lifeline between the city and rest of the country so that troops could overtake the city. Fortunately, they could not hit it and missed it each time. Perhaps we were fortunate, soon Pakistan's army anti-aircraft defense took the alarming situation in control and we watched enemy's aircrafts go down in flames. The petrified screaming turned into applause for the dedicated army but left a permanent mark on our minds, I quivered in fear for several days even after reaching Rawalpindi and meeting my parents. For weeks I woke up screaming in nights and there were times I could not even speak for hours as I had never witnessed death so close before. I missed my home and my life in Lahore. It was all so sudden.

The tension between East and West Pakistan increased day by day. By the time East Pakistan was convinced that forces in West Pakistan will not honor their rightful position in elections and disobedience movement gained strength. Indian army gained control of most of towns in East Pakistan and the history observed the worst bloodbaths where None Eastern citizens in East Pakistan were slaughtered and killed ruthlessly. Young girls were raped, and houses burnt, thousands died and several disabled. Things kept going worse day by day. Every evening there were war sirens which warned civilians to go into hideouts and stay indoors. The male members volunteered to ensure that complete black out was being observed as the enemy fighter planes would bombard any luminous location.

It was as usual morning when the postman brought us a letter from Chittagong (East Pakistan). My brother and her fiancée used to communicate through letters at that time.

Asher, come downstairs,' I called my bother.

What is it?' he asked.

Letter from your bride to be,' I handed over the letter to him. He read the letter and froze in shock. Tears flowed down his eyes in disbelief and sorrow. He was frantically screaming and moaning. His dreams had ended before they even began. His beloved fiancée and her family had become the victims of the brutal riots. The letter was sent by their relative that the entire family has been killed.

Although the violent and blood-shedding war continued only for a few weeks, it ended in complete collapse in communication with our right hand, East Pakistan, breaking up into a separate state now known as Bangladesh. A vast number of families were separated for several years. Those in East could not go to West and those in West could not see their loved ones in East.

The post-war problems were huge. We individually endured the hardships of that war; as a nation we suffered much more. Our nation was fractured socially, damaged economically and diverged politically. Technically we had to build a new Pakistan again, now with its right hand missing.

Since the industries in both parts (East and West) were dependent upon each (for example West Pakistan depended upon East for its jute industry raw material) a lot of economic problems arose after the war. Unemployment increased severely due to shutdown of some major industries. The agricultural sector performance too suffered due to war. This situation leads to rigorous price increases which strongly effected the lives of common people like us.

After a few weeks, I moved back to my city Lahore but it never seemed the same happy place. The brutal war had left a permanent scar on my mind and rotted my soul with hostility. What I simply learnt was that Wars are undignified, horrible and futile. It is man at his very worst.

Testimony Two

I remember seeing quick movements and hearing anxiety in voices and attitudes. I remember that my father came to visit me in the "good lady's" house; where I went for a brief stay, they were cousins, and that was the last time I ever saw him. There were heavy sounds of shelling and bombardments, closer to the city than it had been the for the last two weeks. Many people rushed out into the streets hurrying out of the city – they (we) were evacuating from Port Harcourt.

It happened during the civil war in Nigeria which took place between 1967 and 1970. Port Harcourt, then, was a major city in Biafra and was very strategic in that region of West Africa. The Eastern region of Nigeria seceded and called itself Biafra and was led by Lt. Col. Odemegwu Ojukwu. Nigeria had to fight to keep the country together. Port Harcourt had been besieged for month before it was finally taken over by the Nigerian army.

People were trekking and lamenting the panicky situation. It was a very long trek and lasted for several hours. The roads were littered with properties which people threw away. Many people thought that they could manage to go along with at least food items but it was a wearisome journey and they couldn't cope. Some children were crying amidst hush from their parents to calm them down. I can still remember of a woman who was so frustrated that she voiced out if she should throw away her child. My Cousin told her not to do it. We spent that night in a refugee camp and remained there for some days. One day, a man came with a lorry and carried us away from the refugee camp. We were taken to a village called Aghara near Orlu, in the then Eastern Nigeria. The good Lady I lived with was sheltered in a family friend's house – in a room with her household. I was very young but my mind was able to capture many things around me. I have read stories about the war.

The war which started in 1967, lasted for the next two years. There were a lot of traumatic situations that happened during the war. Biafran soldiers constantly raided the villages looking for food and men to conscript to fight against the Nigerian army. Villagers usually brought out whatever food items they had (of cause not willingly) and the soldiers would carry them away. The soldiers also killed and carried away any domesticated animals like goats, sheep and chickens, they found. Malnutrition soon set in among the civilians populace who were majorly women and children and I was badly affected to the point of almost losing my life. I remember that people hunted rodents and lizards for meat; they did this to supplement for protein. All manner of leaves were eaten and life was a matter of survival, anyhow. Many people, I was told, continued to live in refugee camps and suffered lack of every kind.

Gun men also hunted the villages looking for men who deserted their army formations and fled from the battle, if they found any, they dealt with them in very humiliating manner , they asked them, "who do you want to fight Gowon, if you ran away from the battle?" General Yakubu Gowon was the Nigerian Head of state at that time. Girls as young as ten were abducted by uniformed men. Many other young ladies "join the war"; these were ladies who out of frustration felt that it was safer to go to the soldiers and live with them. One of my distant cousins was one of them. They were not fighting in the war front; they served the army as mistresses to some soldiers, and some others helped in providing whatever care that was needed. After the war, many of them came back ravaged and humiliated.

Many of the young boys and young men who were conscripted into the war never returned. They were ill equipped for such duties and their end was almost predictable. They were not given any training, whatever weapons they had were never going to win a war. At the end of the war, many families hoped endlessly that their loved ones would come back; there were many rumours about spotting some of them; this raised hopes and expectations, but many of them never returned. Their hopes ended in pains, tears and shadows.

One day, late December 1969, there were shouts of joy and relief all over the village, 'the war has ended'; Biafra had lost the war. It was the best thing that happened to people in the past three years that the war raged; though there were mixed feelings, but General Gowon had announced that 'there were no victors, no vanquish'. Some days after that, we were in a lorry heading for Midwest state (as it was known then), to our own town. There were many check-points along the road as we travelled, the military men, (Nigerian military), searched vehicles for what I never got to know; children were not bothered in those searches; girls were hidden behind piles of materials.

I lost my father in that war and my mother was left to bring up six children in conditions that were very challenging. I was told that my father arranged with the lady I was staying with, that morning he came, that he was going to get my family, so that all of us could flee the city together. My family did not show up and we left the city without them. They were held back in the city.

I was never reunited with the whole family, with everyone in there. Some weeks after we returned to my town, the good lady handed me over to my grandfather, who lived in my village; it was a big relief for her. I am sure she would have felt very bad if she had lost me to death. God has spared us and it is a joy for me to be alive to write something about those experiences. I will always remain grateful to her and her family for all their care for me. I will always remain grateful to a lady, Anwuli, who took care of me when I was sick.

I know of people who lost members of their families. There were others who lost some parts of their bodies and many people lost their properties and businesses. I have lived several years charting the course of life and raising my own family, I rarely had time to bother with that period until now that I decided to write about it. I hear of war in many places, terrorist attacks and political skirmishes and I have come to realize that many people don't really know the things wars do to its victims.

After the war, there was a particular incident, where a soldier came to my town, in search of his former mistress; there must have been issues between them, because he ended up killing two young ladies that day before he was apprehended. He claimed one of them was killed as a mistaken identity. There was commotion in the town, we ran back home from school and for days everyone lived in fear that the soldiers might return. The families of those ladies were divested of their loved ones even when the shelling stopped.

I have done well with the help of God. I had opportunities to further my education and gained what is considered reasonable. There were many who never got through the anguishes. Scares last long.

Testimony Three

It was a fine Sunday evening. The sky was blue and was filled with stars conflicting with their twinkling lights; the cold lonely moon gazed down on me. It was indeed a fine evening for a memory. I can't really say why I took time to admire my surroundings. I would have said this night was better than any other nights in South Cotabato, in the past few weeks, except, it that was soon disturbed. No long after my quiet reflection, we were running hastily into the wilderness to save our lives from barbaric killers.

South Cotabato used to be one of the most populous cities in Mindanao, southern part of the Philippine Archipelago. It is surrounded by the city of Sultan Kudarat in the North and West, which is home for the Muslims and encircled by Saranggani Province in the East and South, which is a known Territory for Christians. Contrary to common beliefs and to what is written in many foreign books, news reports and travel advisories, it is not only a home for a certain group of people. It used to be the centre of trade and industry, like what all cities supposed to be, a place where both religion and ideology should not be of any hindrance to growth and progress, until some people started to claim the land for themselves or should I say, wanted it exclusively for themselves and their group; doing all they could to impose their beliefs and faith on other citizens. It was like either an angel of death came one night in their trance and told them to sanitize the land from non-believers or an idea out of insanity just popped up in their minds that made them come and seize other people with the edge of their swords. You know people; if they are not fighting for ideology, gender, status in the society, they go to war for their religion; and to vindicate themselves they come out with a political term to justify their actions: Jihad, Communism, or people's power.

I ran into the house, picked up my younger brother and made for bush. I ran as fast as I could into the endless and thriving wilderness, trying to dodge the stray bullets from their howling rifles that pierced indiscriminately into the air and crashed into the trees; leaving savage souvenirs on their trunks. My five year old brother tightly clutched on my back screening his cries; his tears streaming freely down his face wetting my shoulders. His weight never seemed to bother my fragile ten year old wretched body. I never realized how heavy my brother was; the burden inside my chest was way heavier and real. I estimated I had been running for hours now.

At some point, I wondered how far I got and wanted to take some rest but I never stopped dashing into the hazy darkness. I knew that if I get caught, that would be the end for both of us and our souls will wander restlessly on the earth looking for his bloody member.

The night was lit up like fireworks with fires from explosions and unending shots fired from their high-powered rifles. Calmness was ruined by the blinding blasts of grenades and that would only bring a gloomier future to us. I got worried about my parents who were running beside me and were lost amidst the chaos but I couldn't stop, my feet seemed to be on auto – pilot, on survival mode and could only hope for the best or the worst, whatever comes first. I started to get angry with myself for being a coward, but I was really just a child then, stripped scarring out from my youth; deprived of happy childhood moments.

I felt too much resentment for those people and their kind. I started cursing the people who invented weapons, although, I never knew their names; they were just somebody whom I didn't know and need not to know but whose deed could distress my future. I felt too much hatred with science and religion and ideology. I cursed the stolid trees that blocked my journey to safety. I blamed everything.

The last thing I can remember was when a group of uniformed men met me at the end of the forest. It was already dawning. They were all shouting and firing back at the muddled woods. One man in camouflage and a name plate on his left chest that read Santos took my brother from my back. I looked at my back to check for my parents but I only caught a glimpse of our town at a distance which was then enveloped by an infernal blaze. The thick smoke seemed like a ghost from the dead yesterdays' dreams that flew up to the Creator. It made me felt like crying but no words came out of my gaping mouth, my eyes couldn't even let out tears; that could have made me feel better. Innocence was draining out of my existence. I was exhausted and in a moment passed out. When I woke up, I was at the back of a huge six by six military vehicle with a bunch of my fellow refugees. My mother, who was praying the rosary, sat as if whispering incantations on my left, beside her was a woman whose face was all covered by a black veil muttering indistinctly. My father was sitting in front of me exchanging conversation with an old man with a kippah on his head and counted strands of beard on his chin. I looked up, the sun was already shining on the trees and made their luminous leaves glow. The smell of county grass drenched with the salty breeze and stale blood brought a nostalgic smell and remembrance of the events of last night inside my head. It made my stomach sick and made me want to throw up. Abruptly, I examined my body and looked for wounds and was happy to find none.

Now, I realize that I have deeper and invisible scars inside my heart that throbs every time I gaze on that mocking lonely moon. The sceneries outside the moving truck turned eagerly like pictures and I missed my home. The past should not define the future but its exhausting ashes flows endlessly to my present.

It happened many faded years ago but the anguish and terror are still clear like pictures on a giant screen inside my mind; echoing, bleeding, grinning. The things that had changed my life forever happened so fast yet the recovery had been too slow. My family, although still hurting from the loss, had to move miles and seas away from our hometown trying to escape the war and accepted that we cannot hold on to anything forever. We had to move on and leave the good old days behind, they are now buried beneath those smoking slugs. I still wake up in the middle of the night from countless gnashing nightmares shivering, soaked with cold sweat. The warlords and their new recruits still infest the place until now according to the news; terrorizing and claiming what they called "promise land". The soldiers are still in constant battle to control outbursts of armed conflicts. The sales of weapons and supplies continue to flourish while the values of lives seem to diminish.

There had been a lot of violence from those extremists. A lot of people had be kill, they ravaged their captive women, killed their husbands while shouting with pride as they glory in battles against people they confronted without warning.

Testimony Four

I still feel like it was yesterday, I was only nine years old then. I was a happy child, living in the great neighbourhood in a small town called Sombor, in the north of Serbia. Everything was perfect; I played all kinds of games every day with my friends, until one particular morning when things changed for us.

It was March 14, 1999, I was outside doing what kids do, playing, exploring and just having fun; suddenly I heard some unusual sound and I didn't know what it was. About a minute later, I heard an explosion and it sounded like it was 500m away from me. My friend and I got scared and started running to our homes. Suddenly I saw my father with a scared look on his face, screaming my name. We went in the basement of our building and I was surprised to see almost every tenant there. My brother was in the corner, sitting on some kind of brick. I looked closely, but I couldn't find my mother. I started yelling at my father, asking him where she was.

She was still working. NATO was bombarding our town. It sounds almost impossible to believe that my mother was at work while bombs were destroying our town. I prayed that she will show up unharmed and somehow that miracle happened and I was so happy to see her gain.

In the basement all the parents tried not to bother with the kids. I was really scared. Our building was shaking from the bomb blasts. NATO was bombarding a place 2 km away from us.

Going to the basement became an everyday thing for us. We had a radio that informed us about the bombing and the victims. When there was no siren, we felt safe and tried to continue a normal life; but when we hear that horrible sound, everyone starts to panic and run to the basement.

I remember many nights, waking up scared, not knowing what will happen next; are we going to die? Is the next bomb going to be dropped on our building? What if they drop one on us? Is this how my life is going to end? And what we did do to deserve such a thing? I was not in war, my father was not in war, and my grandfather was not in war. So why was this happening to us? Many question, zero answers.

One day my parents decided it was safer for us to go to our weekend cottage. It was unfinished, but they thought we would be safer there. My grandparents joined us and we all went there. It was a small cottage, outside our town; there was no logic of dropping bombs there, at least my parents thought so. They were wrong.

Not only that, it was freezing cold and planes flying over our cottage. That night everyone was scared. We just had to hold on that night and in the morning, we returned to Sombor. My parents decided that we go to our grandparent`s house. I remember thinking, at least if we die, we will all die together. We stayed there until the bombardments ended. Our president signed some kind of an agreement with NATO. There were no more sirens, no more bombs and worries. I was really happy, but nothing was the same again. I found out that one of my best friends lost his father in that NATO aggression.

As for me, I went back to school pretending like nothing happened; years has passed and still, when I think about that period of time, I get very angry. Everything is rebuilt now, but what about our people? Many innocent people died and why? Politics? And who has the right to take someone`s life? They think that people in Serbia are some kind of animals. I just know one thing; we didn`t deserve this, no one deserves this. I hope that today in the 21st century, people are going to stop killing each other. Unfortunately, I listen and watch the news on the television and what happened to me is still happening somewhere else. Nothing has changed.

Testimony Five

I am a 22 years university student who had a horrid experience of warfare. It was a very horrible experience. I was at the risk of losing my life when I went to Kashmir (India) two years ago. I never thought that I will share my story with others, but one of my best friends encouraged me to share it. That is why I am sharing this story and I hope my readers will understand my feeling at that moment.

I went to Kashmir visit my uncle who has been living in Kashmir for last 12 years. I had been keen on seeing Kashmir; people called "heaven on earth", in my place. I was very excited when we started our journey, it was a dream come true. We travelled for about three hours in the midst of deep silent night and finally we arrived Kashmir in the early hours of the next day. I saw the natural beauty of Kashmir, it appeared to me that it was the really heaven on earth. Kashmir was surrounded by Apple and orange gardens. And the High sloping hills and valleys of Kashmir were very astonishing and it made me wild with excitement. I could not imagine that something a horrific incident was waiting for us.

It was 20th January 2012, at 7 am and we headed for northern Kashmir to see 'Kashmir valley'. My cousin (Mr. Arman) was with me. That day the roads were closed; as tensions increased between the local Muslim soldiers and the Hindus of northern Kashmir. My brother Arafat told me to return home, but I was adamant to go on my visit; I had no ideas about the real situations of that area. Out of the blue, Hindus attacked the Muslim village in the valley. I had never seen a big fight like that. My cousin knew very well what to do in a war situation and said we should run for hiding, fast; we did and took shelter in a mountain side, at the house of a man named Abu Saidi. He prohibited us from going out of the house. The Hindus and Muslims were always fighting each other in that region; both groups used heavy lethal weapons. The clash lasted for about four hours.

Later, the Indian Army took control of the situation. A curfew was imposed that night. So we stayed the whole night there indoors. In that tragic incident about 90 people were killed. It was like a "cursed came down to the 'heaven'". We visited several villages in the next morning, when the army left; many villages were completely destroyed. There were blood stains all over the place and we heard that several women were taken captive. I wandered, where is human feeling; why all this destruction of lives and properties? I saw how ruthless people can be. Thousands of families lost their homes. No one knows how long it would take to make the situation here normal again. Two years had passed; I couldn't forget the incident. I had been haunted by it constantly. That horrible incident made a very bad impact upon my mind which will be hard to erase.

Statistics show that, A huge number of youngsters have been influenced by the clashes in Kashmir. Numerous youngsters are compelled to escape, while many are compelled to pick up the gun themselves; they are standing up to the physical damage, roughness, risk, misuse, alarm and misfortune. The community is polarized and can no more give protection and confidence to youngsters. Schools are constantly interrupted by these clashes. This is my story; it is indeed the real story of my life that I shall never forget.

Testimony Six

It was a typical day for us in the province of Cebu, Philippines in the year 1942. I and my siblings were very busy helping our parents with farming in our corn field. We were all happy then, despite the scarcity of good livelihood. our parents taught us not to focus on material things but to invest in emotions. We grew up in a family were rivalry was not known but sharing and loving each other. One day my father was ploughing our corn field while my mother was busy planting corn. I took care of my two little sisters and two little brothers, since I was the eldest. We kind of joined in the farming in little kids' enthusiasm.

My sisters were planting corn when one of them asked to go to the shrubbery to urinate. Suddenly the Japanese helicopters were flying across the sky and dropping missiles everywhere. We were panicking and running without directions. Houses were burnt and people were dying. The cry for help grew louder but no one could help anyone. There was no hope for everyone around. I late heard that Japanese soldiers were all over beating and killing people that come across their way.

Women were raped and killed. Men became slaves and I was one of them.

The worst scenario that turned our life upside down was that a bomb burned my sister. My other brother was hit by the flashing missile and was injured. He ran to our corn field and shouted for help. We were unable to do much to help him. It was a big pain to my parents. The trauma that it caused was unimaginable. When the shelling stopped we found the bodies of my two siblings; it one of the most difficult things to bear. We buried them in front of our backyard under a big Mahogany tree. We witnessed everything and I cannot contain the emotion ; my parents were devastated.

It had been almost 65 years since but the trauma, tragedies, agony, feelings and the experience are still fresh in my mind and torment me always. I have tried to suppress them and the lessons I've learned will always remain in my heart. I will pass them to my children and grandchildren.

I always told my children not to give up and to pray always for guidance and wisdom. No matter what struggles and problems they may have now, I believe they will go on and succeed in life. I am grateful that I am still alive to tell my story and no one knows when my end time is.

Testimony Seven

On October 29, 1956, three nations began their war against Egypt; Britain, France and Israel. The crisis began as a diplomatic issue, when Gamal Abdel Nassed, the Egypt's president, at that time, made an announcement declaring the nationalization of Suez Canal after Britain and United States refused to fund the building of High Dam in Aswan.

The war, by the Western nations, was aimed at regaining the control of Suez Canal and removing Nasser from presidency of Egypt. The war grew daily and foreign countries bombed Cairo, the capital.

I, Hajj Abdo Mohareb, witnessed the war which took place in 1956. I lived in Suez city, Alarbaeen region near downtown Suez. I have a family of eight; four sons and two daughters.

We were all asleep when we heard the sound of an explosions that sounded like that an earthquake. We all woke up distressed and began moving from our rooms. we went into the street as we thought the house was falling apart.

Just when we went out into the streets, we couldn't believe what we saw. The sky was blinded by airplanes bombing allover Suez without differentiating between civilian districts and army-based territories. We hadn't seen any fight or battles before, we saw our city ruined by fires. The government evacuated of Suez city to other governorates.

We lived nearly two months moving from one shelter to another escaping scourge of war. We first moved to Aladabya near Aladabya port which did not witness the war at first; we stayed there for less than ten days until the forces began to strike Aladabya. We then moved to Ataqa region which was nearly empty at that time. We stayed there for 40 days before we moved to my uncle's house in AlQalubya. We stayed away from Suez for 24 years; we returned to Suez in 1980.

We had not imagined that someday we would not be able to defend our homes, beloved one, our sons or even ourselves. We witnessed friends, brothers and relatives die during war.

Before the war, I was working at Suez port which was partly ruined from air strikes. I had no job; we could not provide ourselves with food, water and clothes. We lived like this for several months.

In AlQalubya, I finally began to work in a farm. At that time I was paid less than 4 piaster per day and that was what I used for our food and daily expenses.

This situation lasted for more than 20 years. It was a time of poverty, suffering and hopelessness. It was frustrating watching your country's resources drained by an occupation army.

There were two other wars; they were basically based on popular resistance in which ordinary people who do not have any skills using fire arms, fought against well-trained soldiers. The Egyptian army distributed fire arms to the public and encouraged them to fight and set up traps for enemy troops. This actually came with unexpected results which reflected the real will, determination and insistence to evacuation the enemy forces from our land. We indeed won a war, but what it did cost us? Youths, money and land.

We came out as losers of the consequent three wars on Egypt. We were affected economically or morally. Wars affected every single Egyptian. In 1967, my cousin, Shaaban, a veteran in the army serving in Kasfareet air base, was killed during the battles which ended with Israel occupying the western side of Suez Canal. The war effected every Egyptian especially those who lived in Canal cities; Suez, Port Said and Ismailia.

Testimony Eight

I was born in a town called Ba Xuyen in Vietnam in 1973 towards the end of the war. My 'mother' told me about the first years after my birth. After I was born, I was left on a doorstep of a church. The church was used as an orphanage for abandoned children. The Catholic priests and nuns running the orphanage had set up a network to take in children, care for them, and find homes for them abroad. I was adopted by an American family in Colorado.

The story of how I arrived in the USA is rather uninteresting. To sum up, after I was healthy enough to travel and they had found a family willing to adopt me, the church ordered a birth certificate with a fictitious name for me, a fictitious parents and presumably an estimation of date of birth and location. With those documents somewhere on my person, I was placed in a wicker basket and handed over to the flight attendants aboard a Pan Am flight headed for Denver, Colorado. Of course, my mom showed me a picture of the Captain walking off the plane with me in my basket. I arrived when I was 11 weeks old.

My childhood seemed rather normal, but what is normal? My parents divorced when I was about 4 or 5 years old. I became accustomed to an only child of a single parent way of life. As I grew up, I realized how different I looked to all the other children. Daily ridicule quickly became the "norm" of my "normal" life. "Remember Pearl Harbor!" was a popular insult yelled at me as I was chased by bigger kids wanting to make sure I got the message. I didn't really understand though. I am not Japanese. What were they talking about?

Sometimes looking different was an advantage and I made friends rather easily. My friends, like any young kids, were curious about me and my origin. However, not knowing much about myself, let alone my history, I made things up. *I created scenarios where I remembered my family in Vietnam. I had brothers and sisters just like my friends did. I wasn't so different from them. Then came the embellishment. This is how I addressed the questions about my "real" family. A bomb landed on my brother while we were eating breakfast and killed him. I saw the whole thing. My whole family was killed during the war and I was the only one to survive. My friends were amazed, so amazed that they had to tell their parents.* I remember my mom telling me that she was getting calls from horrified parents who had heard all of these stories from her adopted son.

As I grew older, the insults became fewer. Kids can be horrific and very mean. My teen years were spent in the 80s and early 90s. This was just before the term, "politically correct", came to be and stereotypes of Asians were in abundant supply. From buckteeth, pocket protectors, slick straight hair, squinty slits for eyes behind big glasses with thick lenses to cameras around the neck always at the ready to capture that unforgettable moment, which happened to be every single moment apparently, I was cautious of the image I was going to portray. Not having grown up in the typical Vietnamese household, I was fully American. I never wanted to be Asian ("oriental" if you remember that age), I was forced to be. So I did everything I could to distance myself from other Asians even so far as to turn away beautiful girls who wanted to date me. The last thing I was going to be was the stereotype. However, no matter how hard I tried, I couldn't escape. People who didn't know me automatically assumed that I bowed at everything, ate rice with every meal, or even worse, dogs and cats. No one would really try to fight me, since it was assumed that every Asian knew how to fight Karate or Kung Fu. I didn't mind that so much.

As I grew older, I went to college, graduated, and became gainfully employed; I started to travel. Most of it was work-related and my jobs often took me into southern Louisiana. I've long considered that part of the U.S. to be the place where education goes to die and modernization as never having arrived. I remember an instance where I was waiting to board a helicopter with my company's clients to go offshore. It was foggy that day and the heliport personnel announced that there would only be one flight. As we pondered who was more critical to operations and would get the ride offshore, one of the client representatives voiced his opinion. Pointing at me he said, "He's the minority. He should stay behind and wait until tomorrow." Unfortunately, that feeling, although not expressed as often or as crudely, was common. What was really disappointing is that it wasn't only from the "good ole boy" Americans.

Southern Louisiana is known for New Orleans, jazz, Bourbon Street, and fresh Gulf of Mexico seafood. Vietnamese people are known to be good fisherman (as well as nail technicians and welders), so there was a rather decent sized Vietnamese community around the areas I used to work. I would see Vietnamese welders or convenience store owners most often. They would all try and speak to me in Vietnamese and I would simply raise my arms and tell them that I don't understand them. That is when the grilling would start. "Why don't you know you language?" I left the "r" off "your" intentionally because that is how they spoke to me. "You need learn Vietnamese."

So, I spent my 20s and 30s thinking about how I would never be 100% accepted by races other than Vietnamese because, well, I'm Vietnamese. And I would never be 100% (or 50% for that matter) accepted by Vietnamese because I hadn't a clue about the culture, the language, the food, or even how to pronounce my own Vietnamese name properly.

Recently, I spoke with the nun whom I thought had found me. She revealed to me more details about how I came to her orphanage. I was, in fact, left on the doorstep of a church but not her church. Through the network developed for war abandoned children, I was discovered and sent to her in hopes of being adopted. I questioned my birth date and how accurate it could possibly be. Growing up, I was always told a specific date, plus or minus 2 weeks. In reality, my birthday could be 4-6 weeks off. By the time I was found and sent to the orphanage near Saigon, several weeks had passed because the infrastructure in the early 70s during a war didn't support simply getting in a car and driving to the next orphanage. Medical testing for age were not reliable and so a date was assigned.

The same sister, with whom I have grown quite close, has written books on the experiences at the orphanage and the stories of some of the children who had come and gone. She had told me that most of the abandoned children had died. I recall reading in her book about a plane carrying more than 300 children who were being flown out of the country had crashed and all lives were lost.

What is the point of this? I suppose it's to convey a message. I was fortunate. I have a loving mother. I was raised well. I have made something of myself. But don't think that there isn't a down side. I don't know my birth parents, if I had siblings, or even my own name or birthday. I can't help a doctor when asked about my medical history. I can't speak with other Vietnamese people or understand them when they talk among themselves after learning about my life. Even though I was raised by a Polish family in

Chicago, I can't fully relate to Caucasians, and will never be considered equal. I can't watch a commercial for Ancestry.com and think anything but, "yeah, not going to work." In terms of lineage, I am the first and may be the last, but at least I know karate or Kung Fu. After all, we all do.

Testimony Nine

Every person has some unbearable bad memories of life. These bad memories and experiences create unhappiness and pain in one's life. Having to live in war zone is the worst thing a man can experience in his life.

Back in 1971, a civil war took place between former WEST PAKISTAN and my beloved motherland Bangladesh. At that time Bangladesh was a province of West Pakistan known as EAST PAKISTAN. We were the majority, but the Pakistan Government did not fulfil our fundamental demands. They took our power, money, wealth, everything. Besides that, they also wanted to change our mother language. Once Pakistan

Army decided to take over our country by heinous as well as unconstitutional way; our people decided to resist them at any cost. When the situation deteriorated a lot of people, including my family left the capital city and moved to the villages for safety. At that time every house were robbed, innocent women and children were raped and slaughtered in cold blood.

The former Indian Prime Minister, Indira Gandhi, supported us to fight back to be free from West Pakistan. During the war many unforgettable thing happened to me. My father was a freedom fighter who fought for our homeland. The Pakistan Army sought to capture him at that time. Once, a troop of Pak Army came to our village to catch red handed some of our freedom fighters including my father. My father was informed of this beforehand and he came to the house to move our family to another place quickly; anyway we escaped from home before the army came. My father run away from the village after keeping us in one of our neighbour's house. As a little boy, I was frighten to talk or cry, I just saw what was going on then. At midnight some soldiers of Pak army came to the house and looking for my father. They ransacked the house but did not find him. When they could find him, they became angry; and vandalized the whole house, demolished all of our furniture and household things. They slaughtered our cattle and robbed our valuable things. A couple of grenades were blast explored by them. When they left, they burnt all parts of our house. We all watched their brutal works from a distance. The next morning when we came back to our house it was in ruins. Only a little valuable information saved our life that night, otherwise we were dead. After nine months of fierce fight, we got our freedom after defeating the Pakistan army. At last we got a free and sovereign country. But that horrible night's memory has always been a nightmare to me. I tried several times to forget that horrible night, but I couldn't. Sometimes fear grips me at night while asleep. I have been very much affected by that war mentally and physically as a little boy and now after many year. War is simply a waste of money, time and lives. Nobody could ever convince me otherwise. Some people don't want peaceful solutions. Their rude behavior and greediness to hold on to power bring sufferings to the people. Most of the political leaders always try to grab power in heinous ways. They don't care about people's sufferings or fate.

Are we really going to learn from the wars? I think we are not learning from wars. Our leaders are always trying to impose their wrong and unrealistic decisions on the people which creates anarchy and unpleasant condition in the country. Everybody should remember why we fought for freedom, fought for development, fought for our own language, fought for our rights. We should remember our people who gave their lives for the freedom of the country. We should remember and salute 2.5 lakh (100,000) women who were raped by Pakistan army. If our leaders try uphold these valuable contributions, then we can build a prosperous country.

I wish our country as well as the whole world will be more peaceful and safe for our children to live.

Testimony Ten

My brother and I could not resist wailing on the news that our loving mother and two sisters were among the hapless in the horrendous massacre. For once, I thought that the news were a total crap of fiction. This, as a certain local politician would later put, could *only be possible in a movie*. Or what else would be said of the sight of several authentic human beings, my close relatives included, getting roasted in a church hall?

I was only 14, when hell broke loose in Kenya. The 27th of December 2007—a day no Kenyan will ever forget-- had been appointed as the election's day. I could hear my father argue with his friends on how tight the elections were. Political analysts predicted a *'neck-to-neck'* race in the presidential elections. A vocal politician, Raila Odinga, had gained great influence at the Coast, Rift Valley and the highly populous western provinces of the country. His Orange Democratic Party (ODM) was gaining euphoria, sweeping mightily across the nation's electorate. Pre-election polls predicted that ODM had a chance of trouncing the President Mwai Kibaki-led Party of National Unity (PNU).

No sooner had the campaigns started than they took a different angle. Politicians from both parties resulted into toiling resiliently to garner votes from their respective tribes. They worked to fulfil the Darwinian philosophy of *'survival-for-the-fittest'*. But unfortunately, they fell to 'the trick of the devil' by incorporating provocative remarks to enhance the eloquence of their speeches. They perennially incited people along their tribal lines. Vernacular media houses shelved objectivity and were often heard egging on animosity against tribes that were opposed to their political views. Songs, speeches and news production was evidently meant to fuel a perilous political rivalry.

Tension rose so high that it could be felt. The grapevine had it that there would be mass evictions and displacement if a certain party failed to win.

Tutaondoa madoadoa (We shall remove the spots)," I heard some neighbours rant.

On 27th December 2007, our mum prepared breakfast at 4pm – two hours earlier than she was used to. Schools had closed for the December festivals and thus, it was unusual for anyone to wake up at such a dawn. It was the electioneering day. My parents and elder brother drove to Cheptiret polling station to cast their votes. As teachers by profession, my parents were privileged to own a car. Economically, we were arguably among the best families in the village. Little did we know that this would cost us so much grief later …

My two little sisters and I were left in the house. When we woke up, I rushed to catch up with the news. Countrywide trepidation filled the air. Nairobi, the capital and Eldoret my home city particularly received heavy surveillance from the police, owing to their dense population and volatile history of election-related crimes.

It took three days for the final elections to be announced. I articulately remember how the names of the presidential candidates were stated by the presiding officer. But the climax of a month old tension was reached climax when Mwai Kibaki was announced as the winner.

It was on a Sunday -I remember the day so well-when the chairman of the electoral commission finalized announcing the results and President Kibaki was sworn in the same evening. But it was as if that was a spell of doom to our lives. Supporters of ODM believed that their rivals had rigged the elections. Kalenjins, who were the major tribe in the area, and

Kikuyus were involved in a horrendous tribal clash. Kalenjins supported ODM while the Kikuyu were pro-PNU.

My mind cannot escape the shocking sight of smoke from a neighbor's house. Assailants had burnt it down. Our house remained untouched until after four days. Before the elections, I had not necessarily known that I was of Kikuyu descent. All along, we had lived harmoniously with our neighbors the Kalenjin. In fact, most of my friends were Kalenjin children. We spoke Kiswahili and seldom used our mother tongues.

But all these changed radically on this particular day. It was around 10pm when our house was torched. I can only recall seeing my mother crying. Our father, our good loving dad, had been pierced severally with spears. My brother rushed him to the Moi Teaching and Referral Hospital in Eldoret town. This was the most disheartening sight I had ever seen. But, the worst was yet to come.

We were homeless. My little sisters cried helplessly. Though police came to contain the situation, they seemed biased towards their respective tribes. They could either join the assailants in looting or turn a blind eye.

We thought we were safe until the assailants came back. This time around, they were not just ready to burn houses. They were determined to kill anyone who was not from their tribe. Women were raped, girls were molested, men were maimed, and properties was looted or burnt to ashes. A cloud of melancholy engulfed the whole village. For once, I asked: "Was it wrong that I was born a Kikuyu?"

We stood clueless. My mother and a few neighbors resolved to flee to a neighboring church hall. In the wisdom of all of us, this was the safest place one could ever hide. The Kenya Assemblies of God (KAG)-Kiambaa church was situated about a kilometer from our village. We walked hurriedly to the place, fearing that the assailants would ambush us. We met more people there. The ethnic clashes had brought together people from as a far as Kesses, a town 10km from the area. We all spent the night there.

After rushing dad to the hospital, Kamau, my brother joined us at the church. He had been directed by one of his loyal friends. He told us about how the ruthless killers had blocked roads. They maimed everyone whose language did not rhyme well with theirs. My brother had all stars to thank for his knowledge of the Kalenjin language. When the asylum-seekers talked, one could not help but weep as they narrated the terrific memories of how their relatives had been mutilated.

We spent a night in the church that Monday night, about a week after the announcement of the election results. Early in the morning, for what I never discern whether to call it a revelation or intuition for salvation, my brother and I went to check on our maimed dad. I remember that Tuesday morning, as if it were yesterday; how I unusually and *un-African-ly* hugged mum and my lovely sisters. They looked at me and innocently called my name, "Sam, bye…"

My brother's knowledge of the Kalenjin worked splendidly in our favor. We were able to pass all barricades that the goons had set up on the busy highway. At the Moi University Teaching and Referral Hospital (MTRH), I met my dad and he was recuperating fast. The spear-wounds at his abdomen had been bandaged.

My teenage curiosity glued me to the television screens in the hospital ward. Longing for peace, I always felt urged to know what was happening in the country. But the scenes that appeared on TV were disheartening. Broadcasts were mainly covered with nothing but horrors of Kenyans killing each other. The situation had grown to an ethnocide. In less than a week, Kenya had villainously rebranded itself from Africa's most stable state to a reincarnation of the Holocaust.

But that was not long before it was reported that attackers had killed at least 35 women and children in the Kenya Assemblies of God Church in Kiambaa, Eldoret. The news made my knees lose verve,-I fell on the floor. This was the same church hall that I had left my mother and two juvenile sisters. To add pepper to the story, horrible scenes- of how children were thrown back to the furnace after their parents tried to save them- were shown. It was horror of the vilest order.

Panic set in, my brother phoned several people to inquire about the state of our mum and siblings. The few who had survived confirmed-that indeed, our mother and two sinless sisters had died… This is a memory I would love to erase, but forgetting seems the hardest thing I can ever do.

Well, years have passed. My dad is now better but walks on clutches. We now live on a land where the government settled us; me, my dad and other Internally Displaced Persons (IDPs). We lived in a prestigious mansion, but now, a wooden house is our sojourn.

My once rich dad is now handicapped and depends on me and my brother for support. Our wealth was reduced to this – nothing.

But Kenya has now gained stability (and political maturity too). With the dreadful effects of the war that left almost 2,000 dead and hundreds of thousands displaced, everyone seems mindful. Nowadays, Kenyans are united in the fight against the Al Shabaab extremist terrorists.

Chapter Four

Conclusions

Armed Conflicts and wars are as old as the world. Every day weapons are produced in large quantities, people are recruited and trained in readiness for war. These are indications that people will continue to fight wars.

Many efforts have been made to reduce and minimise armed conflicts. The United Nations and many other organisations do so much to see that peace prevails when there is a likelihood of war in any part of the world. Many armed conflicts especially in underdeveloped countries occur and escalate before any opportunity for peace could be explored; many of them are so because those spearheading the conflicts are short-sighted and arrogant. There are selfish motives behind the carnages that we see every day.

There are many people who want to help the gods win the world through wars and armed conflicts. Many religions and their leaders see 'unbelievers' as enemies who must be eliminated to make their world a better place. Why would the gods live in peace and allow mortal humans to fight for them? There are many people suffering in silence because of what they suffered as a result of armed conflicts no matter how small. They become bitter and vow to retaliate if they have the opportunity to do so. Many warmongers are unrepentant and bitter, win or lose, they never forget or forgive. Their anger never gets pacified. War is a form of bullying at a large scale. The situation of the world has always been that the strong rule the weak. This has always been resisted and what follows is usually bitter bloodletting as we see everywhere today.

From the experiences shared in this book, it is clear that people everywhere suffers because of war. They suffer pains that are difficult to express, hard to forget and are followed by shadows that refuses to go away.

Attempt to enslave people in any form, politically, economic, religious or socially will potentially lead to conflict with time.

People who are wilfully denied their rights, will one day take up arms to fight injustice.

We can rise up against war; nothing is too small to do. When the public rose up against the conflicts in Iraq in 2003, the situation changed. According to The Telegraph, Feb. 2003, "Britain witnessed its largest demonstration yesterday when an estimated one million protesters took to the streets of London to oppose the looming war against Iraq…thousands of demonstrators carried banners with messages such as "No War On Iraq" and "Make Tea, Not War". The crowds at two starting points on the Embankment and Gower street were so large that the police began to march early for safety reason" "Large peace protests were also held all over the country and around   the   world." (http://www.telegraph.co.uk/news/uknews/142228 - One million march against war)

Warmongers can label us as "cowards", if we question the rationale behind the quest for war. They may label us as 'rebels' if we ask for what other options there might be but our rights are as much as theirs and if our lives are on the line, fight or not; if we know that we or our loved one may run the risk of pain or even death during and after the conflict, then our rights to know the details must be respected.

Many leaders want more territory while they cannot adequately care for the ones under them. There are many politicians whose attitudes are "if I don't win, then lets break up". Dichotomy owing to intolerance and at the expense of human lives, is rash and should be rejected.

Freedom of speech and choice of who to serve as God should be respected. Let those propagating ideologies and religion present their arguments and give people the right to decide what to do. Going to war to fight for converts cannot make a good convert. Worship is of the heart and the beauty of worship is out of a sincere and pure heart. Majority of people who testified in this book had occasions of questioning the existence of God. This is borne out of the evils they saw and felt as a result of avoidable wars.

According to the Red Cross, "The effect of war can continue long after people stop shooting." The Red Cross listed some of the impact of a conflict when the shooting has stopped as

- The changed lives of those who have lost family and friends

- The changed lives of those whose family or friends are missing
- Injuries to people and damage to building, system and social structures
- Continuing deaths and injuries from weapons that remain active, such as landmines or shell that failed to explode. These are often grouped together in the technical term unexplored ordnance, or UXO" (British Red Cross, 2004, Life after War)

Wars are not as easy as many people are made to believe. Many ugly sides of armed conflicts are never revealed and it takes years to rebuild, mend or naturalise effects of war. Many people suppress what they feel to their own detriment and the damage continues unabated.

There should be facilities and clinics provided to cater for war victims irrespective of whether they are military personnel or civilians. In recent years, former military men in America, ran rampage, got crazy, killed many people and killed themselves. We may never get to know what happens in individual families of these people, where side-effects of war may be causing pains, tears and shadows. The clinics should not be available only in developed countries but anywhere where there was armed-conflict. Many hospitals might not be well equipped with personnel with the right training to treat war victims and this leaves sufferers susceptible.

The responsibility to rebuild damaged structures, businesses and personal properties should be borne by the authorities and governments. People and foreign agencies should not be saddled with the sole responsibilities of restoring normal life to the communities ravaged by war.

Presently the brunt of health care, food and social wellbeing in underdeveloped and developing countries, who engaged in arm conflicts, are borne by humanitarian and donor agencies, usually from outside warring countries. This should not be so, there must be some joint efforts from within and outside those countries, to help those affected by war to build back their lives.

The promised havens that were used as propaganda before and during the war, as evident in many countries, never materialises. It is a travesty. In most cases, especially in third world countries, corruption sets in sooner after the war and decay is the ultimate.

War can cause many people to flee their countries and seek refuge elsewhere. Sometimes, there are language and cultural differences and it takes a long time to adjust. Many refugees are ill-equipped for this new experience and struggle for a long time. While they are grateful for the benevolence shown to them, they keep longing for home. In some cases, many of the countries harbouring them find it difficult to support them in many meaningful ways because of poor economy and infrastructures.

Join to make a difference and say, "no more wars".

.

Reference

1. United Nations Declaration On Human Right - http://www.un.org/en/documents/udhr/) [Accessed 9th May 2014]

2. Causes of War: http://uk.ask.com, [Accessed 9th May 2014] http://wiki.answers.com [Accessed 9th May 2014]

3. William Little, PeaceMatters: www.ppu.org.uk) [Accessed 9th May 2014]

4. UNICEF: Children in conflict Nov. 2012- Effects of war on children

5. Lucinda March, 2004. Common Dreams, Unacceptable: The Impact of War on Women and Children. (CommonDreams.org, December 18, 2004.) [Accessed 12th May 2014]

6. Much Butchery, 2014, Civilians in war zone, The Economist Newspaper [Accessed 10th May 2014]

7. Anirudh Purwar, Arnab Dhabal and Diptarka Chakravarty: Psychological effects of War and Terrorism on children

8. BBC News, Friday May 9, 2014 (Accessed 9th May 2014)

9. One million march against war – (http://www.telegraph.co.uk/news/uknews/142228) [Accessed 10th May 17, 2014]

10. British Red Cross, 2004, Life after War

11. Cyprian Ekwensi, 1976, Survive the peace, Heinemann.

www.ingramcontent.com/pod-product-compliance
Lightning Source LLC
Chambersburg PA
CBHW060207290526
45789CB00003B/1200